DISCOVER

HAWAI'I'S

BIRTH BY FIRE

VOLCANOES

Midway Islands

Kure Atoll

Pearl and Hermes Atoll

Laysan Island

Maro Reef

Lisianski Island

Gardner Pinnacles

Pacific

Published and distributed by

ISLAND HERITAGE™
P U B L I S H I N G
A DIVISION OF THE MADDEN CORPORATION

94-411 Kō'aki Street, Waipahu, Hawai'i 96797-2806

Orders: (800) 468-2800 • Information: (808) 564-8800

Fax: (808) 564-8877

islandheritage.com

ISBN#: 1-59700-849-4

Second Edition, Eighth Printing - 2017

COP 160812

Copyright ©2009 Island Heritage Publishing

DISCOVER
HAWAI'I'S
BIRTH BY FIRE
VOLCANOES

Written by Katherine Orr and Mauliola Cook

Illustrated by Katherine Orr

CONTENTS

INTRODUCTION

Welina mai i Hawai'i nei.
    —Welcome to the Hawaiian Islands.

A golden red fountain shoots skyward as tons of liquid rock burst from the earth with a deafening roar. The hot air crackles with energy and burns with the sharp smell of sulfur. Glowing rivers of fire pour from the open mouth of the mountain and rush down its black slopes in brilliant fingers of light. Few sights can match the power and beauty of this grand, fiery display—this sight of Mother Nature in the act of creation.

ANCIENT HAWAIIAN LEGENDS

The first Polynesian settlers must have been very impressed by the awesome nature of Hawai'i's volcanoes as they rumbled and roared, spurting forth rivers of hot, liquid lava. These people were first-hand witnesses to the growth of the islands as lava poured out of the earth, covering existing forests and beaches, creating new land as it flowed down the mountain slopes into the sea. Yet, the ancient Hawaiians did not usually think of volcanoes as the creative source that formed their islands. Hawaiian legends, passed from parents to children in the form of chants and stories, express many different beliefs about how the Hawaiian Islands came to be.

The Kumulipo, one of Hawai'i's most well-known chants of creation, speaks of a time when all was hot, the sun darkened, and slime was the source of the earth. Other legends say that Hawaiian gods gave birth to the islands. While some

stories say that certain islands were born of Papa, the Earth Mother, others say that the islands were shaped by the hand of the Sky Father, Wākea.

A favorite legend speaks of Maui, the well-known Polynesian hero, who is said to have pulled the Hawaiian Islands out of the sea with a magic fishhook. While Maui was busy with his magical fishing adventure, his brothers were paddling the canoe. They had been given strict orders not to look back as they paddled, but one brother could not resist temptation. When he turned to look, the giant land mass that Maui was pulling out of the sea fell back into the ocean and only the Hawaiian Islands remained, standing as separate peaks above the waves.

When we think of volcanoes in Hawai'i, there is one name that comes to mind, making us imagine fiery red explosions and glowing golden lava flows. That name—Pele—has been honored by chanters and dancers of hula throughout the islands for hundreds of years. Legends say that Pele sailed to Hawai'i from her homeland in far-off Kahiki, accompanied by members of her family and her sacred digging stick, Pāoa. When their canoe reached the shores of the Hawaiian Islands, Pele and Pāoa began to dig huge craters, searching for the "fires of life" that Pele and her family needed to make their home. When they finally reached the Big Island of Hawai'i, they were happy to find the burning crater pits of Kīlauea and Halema'uma'u. This was indeed a perfect home for the Pele family.

'Ai lā'au, The Forest Eater, was the much dreaded god who ruled over these fire pits, but he was no match for the powerful Pele. After losing to Pele in battle, the defeated 'Ai lā'au ran away and was never heard from again. And so Pele claimed the land for herself. Even today, many Islanders regard Pele with love and respect. They honor her as the great force behind both the destruction of forests, and the creation of new land and beautiful, black-sand beaches.

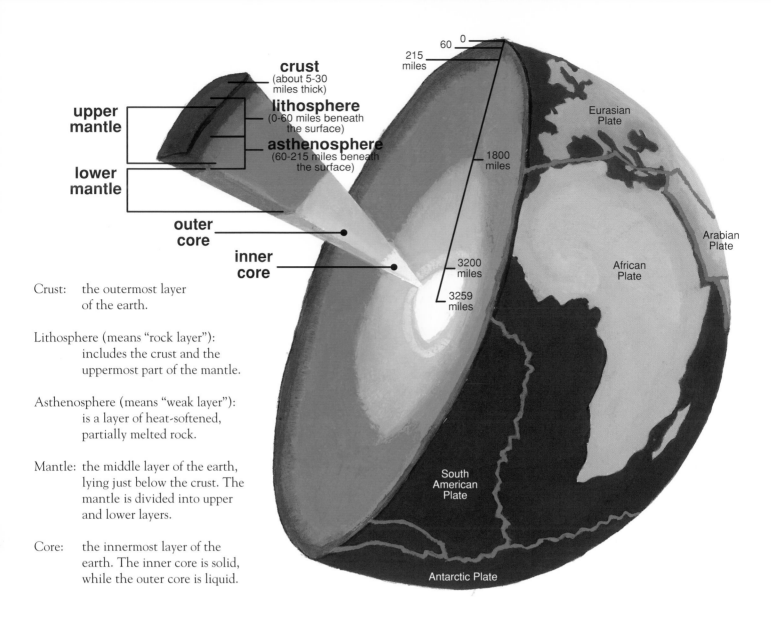

crust
(about 5-30 miles thick)

lithosphere
(0-60 miles beneath the surface)

asthenosphere
(60-215 miles beneath the surface)

upper mantle

lower mantle

outer core

inner core

0
60
215 miles
1800 miles
3200 miles
3259 miles

Eurasian Plate

Arabian Plate

African Plate

South American Plate

Antarctic Plate

Crust: the outermost layer of the earth.

Lithosphere (means "rock layer"):
          includes the crust and the uppermost part of the mantle.

Asthenosphere (means "weak layer"):
          is a layer of heat-softened, partially melted rock.

Mantle: the middle layer of the earth, lying just below the crust. The mantle is divided into upper and lower layers.

Core: the innermost layer of the earth. The inner core is solid, while the outer core is liquid.

EARTH'S CRUST IN MOTION

How do these ancient legends compare with modern scientist' views about the birth of Hawai'i? Here are some of the amazing stories that scientists have to tell.

They speak about giant plates that are constantly moving, and about a "Ring of Fire" that surrounds our Pacific Ocean. Scientists tell us that the surface of the earth is made of a thin layer of hard rock called the "lithosphere," that rests on a thick layer of heat-softened, partially melted rock called the "asthenosphere." Slow movements of hot rock within the earth, cause cracks in the earth's lithosphere that separate it into plates. Scientists say the earth's lithosphere is made up of seven huge plates and several small ones. Although it is very difficult to notice, these plates are in constant slow-motion. How slow is their motion? Try watching your fingernails grow. Although you cannot see them growing, you know they grow because after a while you need to trim them. The earth's plates move about as slowly as your fingernails grow—from less than half an inch per year to more than four inches per year.

The plates rub and grind against each other as they are carried on the slowly moving asthenosphere. Along some edges, new crust is formed as magma (melted rock) pushes to the surface where two plates are separating. Along other edges, old crust disappears as one plate slides beneath another and the lower plate partially melts back into magma.

The Pacific plate, which is almost as large as the entire Pacific Ocean, is slowly moving toward the northwest. This movement occurs as hot magma pushes to the surface along the plate's southeastern edge and hardens into new crust. Along its northwestern edge, the Pacific plate is sliding beneath its neighboring plates and old crust is partially melting back into the mantle. The borders between all the earth's plates are areas of earthquake and volcanic activity. The Pacific Ocean has so many active volcanoes around its edges that this area is called the "Ring of Fire."

But what about Hawai'i? One look at the map shows us that the Hawaiian Islands are not located near the edges of any plates. Instead, Hawai'i's volcanoes are located in the center of the vast Pacific plate. The hot spot theory explains how this can be so...

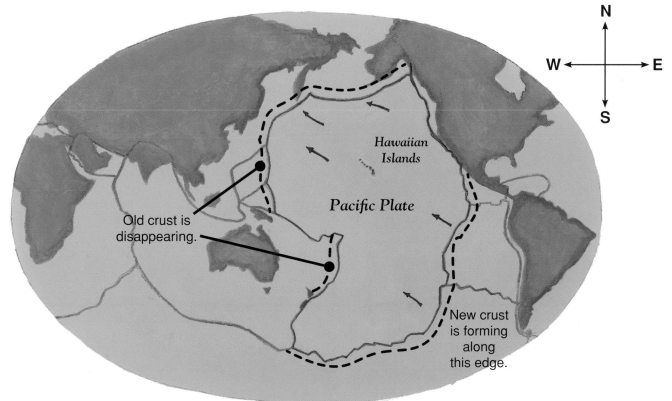

Scientists have discovered that the Pacific plate, as well as other plates in the earth's crust, are renewing themselves slowly all the time. Along its southeastern edge, the Pacific plate is growing as new magma rises to the surface and forms new crust. Along its northwestern boundary, the Pacific plate is slipping beneath its neighboring plate. Once it slips below the surface, the hard rock of the crust melts back into magma.

Rising magma forces its way into the earth's crust. Where it cannot push aside hard rock, the magma collects and pressure increases. From time to time, pressure is released as magma escapes to the surface in volcanic eruptions.

Over a time-span of nearly 70 million years, a hot spot within the earth has produced the 3,500 mile long Emperor Seamount-Hawaiian Island chain.

As new crust is formed at one end of the Pacific plate and old crust is destroyed at the other end, the Hawaiian Islands are moved steadily northwestward, like suitcases carried along a conveyor belt at the airport baggage claim area.

Niʻihau

Kauaʻi (almost 6 million years old)

HOT SPOT UNDER HAWAIʻI

When you heat a pot of water on the stove, you can see currents of water rising and falling within the pot. These currents are created as some patches of water become hotter than their surroundings and rise to the surface, pushing aside cooler water. Similarly, the core, or center of the earth, is a heat source that causes heated rock to rise up through the mantle, or middle layers of the earth, and partially melt in the asthenosphere. Then, magma rises until it works its way through the earth's crust. When the magma reaches rock that is too hard to push aside, it collects and builds up pressure, like an expanding balloon. Finally, the pressure becomes so great that the magma breaks through to the earth's surface in a volcanic eruption. Again and again, magma builds up pressure below the earth's surface, then releases it as a volcanic eruption. Such places where currents of hot magma rise from deep within the earth are called "hot spots."

As hot magma—called "lava" once it comes out of the earth—contacts the cold water of the deep ocean, it cools and hardens into solid rock. In eruption after eruption, layer upon layer of lava pours out of the earth. The layers of lava pile higher and higher, slowly building a mountain under the sea. Eventually, after hundreds of thousands of years, this hot spot volcano grows large enough to rise above the sea. An island is born.

A hot spot is the source of the Hawaiian Islands. Imagine it as a giant fire within the earth that has built a volcano above itself that is tall enough to become an island. The hot spot continues to build the island larger—until the Pacific plate, constantly moving toward the northwest at a speed of about four inches per year, carries the island off the hot spot. Then, a new volcano begins to form over the hot spot. It continues to grow until the moving plates carries it off the hot spot as well. As

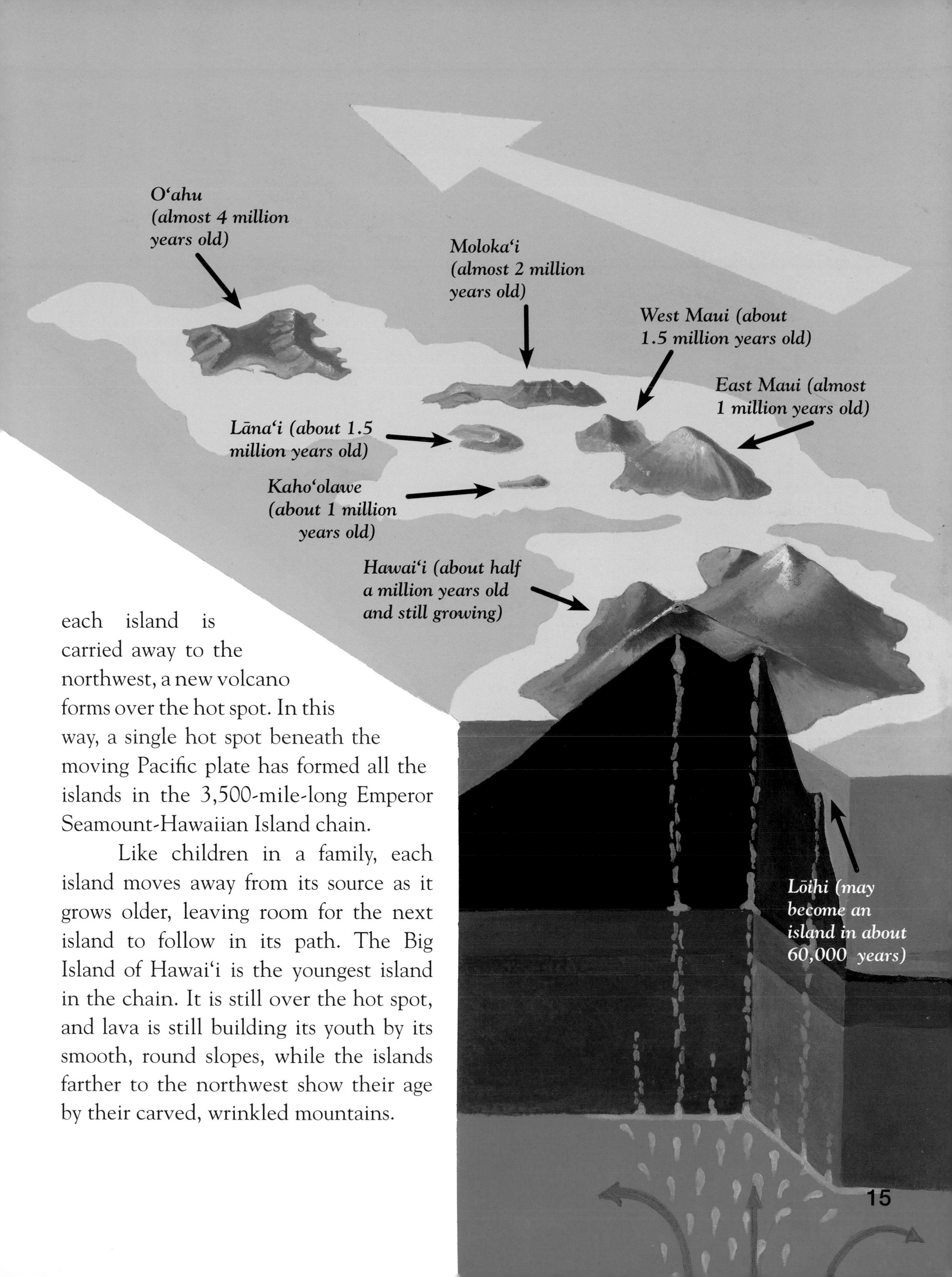

O'ahu
(almost 4 million
years old)

Moloka'i
(almost 2 million
years old)

West Maui (about
1.5 million years old)

East Maui (almost
1 million years old)

Lāna'i (about 1.5
million years old)

Kaho'olawe
(about 1 million
years old)

Hawai'i (about half
a million years old
and still growing)

Lōihi (may
become an
island in about
60,000 years)

each island is carried away to the northwest, a new volcano forms over the hot spot. In this way, a single hot spot beneath the moving Pacific plate has formed all the islands in the 3,500-mile-long Emperor Seamount-Hawaiian Island chain.

Like children in a family, each island moves away from its source as it grows older, leaving room for the next island to follow in its path. The Big Island of Hawai'i is the youngest island in the chain. It is still over the hot spot, and lava is still building its youth by its smooth, round slopes, while the islands farther to the northwest show their age by their carved, wrinkled mountains.

15

Halema'uma'u Crater

THE NEW ISLAND: A WARRIOR'S SHIELD

The volcanoes that form the Hawaiian Islands, as well as volcanoes that are formed by other hot spots around the world, are called "shield volcanoes" because their shape is wide and gently rounded, like the curve of a warrior's shield. The cause of this gently rounded shape is that hot basalt—the lava rock that forms shield volcanoes—flows for a long time and distance before it cools. Thus, mountains built by basalt lava have long, very gently sloping sides. Lava often erupts from shield volcanoes in beautiful fountains of fire. Such eruptions are usually not very explosive because gases that are trapped within hot basalt can escape easily.

Stratovolcanoes, on the other hand, are found along the Ring of Fire where the earth's plates meet. Stratovolcanoes erupt less often and for shorter periods than do shield volcanoes, but their eruptions are more dangerous. They usually have violent, explosive eruptions that are very

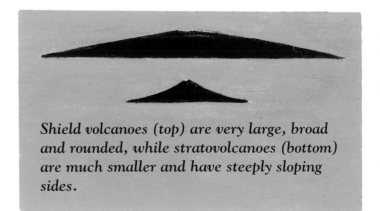

Shield volcanoes (top) are very large, broad and rounded, while stratovolcanoes (bottom) are much smaller and have steeply sloping sides.

Mauna Loa Shield

Kīlauea Crater

destructive to humanity. Both Mt. Fuji in Japan and Mt. St. Helen in Washington state are stratovolcanoes.

The bowl-shaped opening from which lava flows during an eruption is called a "crater." As the volcano grows older, the crater at its top may enlarge and deepen, forming a caldera. This happens because the hard rock of the crater bowl rests on a pocket of liquid magma. If magma erupts from another part of the volcano, often nothing is left to support the heavy rock of the crater. Parts of the crater then collapse, forming a caldera. The caldera grows larger with each collapse.

During some eruptions, lava bursts forth from an opening in the earth and shoots into the sky. The lava that falls to earth around the opening piles up, forming a cone. Scientists give cones names such as "cinder," "spatter," "tuff," and "ash," that describe how they were formed or what they are made of. Although most shield volcano eruptions are gentle, when an eruption occurs near the sea, hot magma sometimes mixes with sea water to create steam. Steam causes explosive eruptions that break the lava into small pieces of ash. The crescent-shaped island of Molokini (off Maui), Crater Hill (on Kauaʻi), and Diamond Head (on Oʻahu) are examples of cones that were made by such eruptions.

Cinder and spatter cones (left) are tall with a narrow crater because they form from deep explosions that shoot lava straight up. Ash and tuff cones (right) are wider with a larger crater because they form from surface explosions that blast lava upward and outward.

LAVA'S CREATIONS

Because the island of Hawai'i is young and still growing, scientists and other visitors come from around the world to see and study volcanoes in action. Here, visitors can examine some of the strange and wonderful creations that are formed by lava as the forces of Pele do their work.

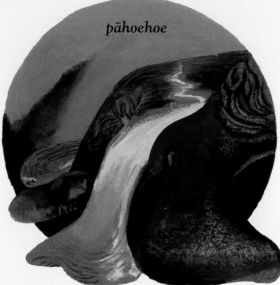

pāhoehoe

'a'ā

FLYING LAVA

During an eruption, some lava piles up into cones, while other lava is flung far through the air. These flying chunks of lava, called "bombs," are named for their different shapes.

FLOWING LAVA

Flowing lava is also named for the way it looks. Lava that looks smooth and glossy, almost like cake batter when it is poured into a pan, is called "pāhoehoe." Lava that has a rougher, gravelly surface is known as "'a'ā." The hot, liquid lava that first flows out of the mountain is pāhoehoe. As the pāhoehoe travels down the mountain slopes, it loses gases and cools. The cooling lava flows more slowly and is stirred up and tumbled as it travels over the rough ground. In this process, the pāhoehoe gradually becomes 'a'ā. On the island of Hawai'i, you can walk right up to hardened flows of pāhoehoe and 'a'ā.

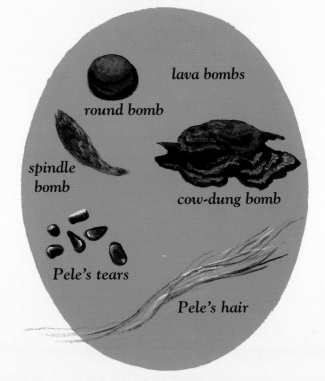

lava bombs

round bomb

spindle bomb

cow-dung bomb

Pele's tears

Pele's hair

Round, spindle, and ribbon bombs are formed by lava that hardens before it hits the ground. Bombs that hit the ground while still fluid are known as pancake or cow dung bombs. Pele's tears are small, drop-shaped bits of lava. Pele's hair is created when fine glassy threads of liquid lava harden in the air. Sometimes, Pele's hair is carried by the wind for miles.

TREE MOLDS

As rivers of pāhoehoe flow down the hillsides, they pass through forests and surrounding living trees. The flowing lava hardens around the tree, leaving behind a mold of the tree. The high heat can cause the wood to burn away, so that the tree molds are hollow. Other tree molds still surround the remains of the tree. If you visit Lava Tree Park in Pāhoa, Hawai'i, on a moonlit night, you will see how very spooky these lava statues look—like frozen ghosts of the forest.

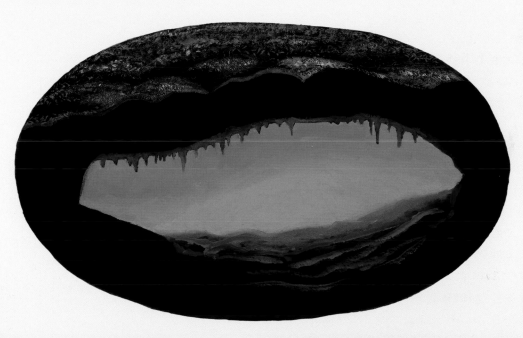

LAVA TUBES

Often, the outer layers of fast-flowing pāhoehoe cool and harden into a crust, while the inside continues to flow like a river. When the crust is thick enough, a hollow tube, called a "lava tube," remains even after the river of flowing lava has drained away. An empty lava tube can be so hot inside that melting lava drips from the ceiling. As the drips cool, they harden into icicles of rock that are known as stalactites.

LIFE COMES TO THE ISLANDS

Hawai'i's newly born islands were black and barren when they first reached above the sea, with no lush green valleys or forested mountains. Where did all the trees come from? How did the wonderful tropical plants that now cover these islands get there? There are only two ways plants and animals can reach an island: by air or by sea. The first plants probably arrived from other Pacific islands as seeds that were either swept along the ocean currents to Hawai'i shores, blown in by the wind, or carried by drifting logs or birds.

Some birds and insects were no doubt blown in by storms. Baby spiders may also have arrived by air, as well as on drifting tree trunks that carried other small animals such as tree snails and crickets. Most of the marine animals that inhabit the shallow seas around Hawai'i today—such as sea urchins, fish, crab, lobsters, and corals—have probably descended from animals that arrived as larvae (babies), drifting with the ocean currents.

People first reached Hawai'i by sailing from their homelands across the sea. They brought with them dogs, pigs, chickens, and many plants. Since then, people have brought many new forms of life to Hawai'i in a very short time, changing the landscape and nature of Hawai'i forever.

Most forms of life that reach a new island do not survive because they find nothing but barren lava rock exposed to the hot sun. Very few plants can live in such conditions, where there is little shade, water, soil, or shelter from wind. But, gradually, as early arrivals settle in the right places and begin to grow, they create shade and shelter so that other, more delicate, plants can survive as well. Over time, the forces of nature break down the rock into minerals that plants can use. Dead leaves and other plant materials collect on the ground and rot, enriching the soil for more plants to enjoy. Very slowly, plants create gentler surroundings in which more plants and animals can live. A web of life slowly forms, as the variety of plants and animals that can live on the island increases.

Tiny coral animals arrive on ocean currents and settle on the hard, black lava slopes of the volcanic island below sea level. Very slowly, these coral animals grow to form coral reefs. In much the same way that various plants growing together over time can develop into a forest, corals growing together over time develop into coral reefs. These reefs, like forests, create food and shelter for a great many plants and animals.

THE ISLAND SHOWS ITS AGE: GRAVITY, WEATHERING, AND EROSION

Even while the volcanic island is still growing in the places where flowing lava builds new land, other parts of the island are starting to age, or break down.

Basalt, the lava rock that forms the Hawaiian Islands, is broken down very easily. Heavy tropical rains, strong winds, and the roots of trees pushing through soil and rocks all help break down basalt. As rainwater mixes with carbon dioxide in the air, it forms an acid that causes minerals in rocks to dissolve. The iron in rocks combines with oxygen in the air to form rust. Just as rust destroys cars and bicycles, it also destroys rocks. If you live in Hawai'i, you know that we have lots of rain, wind, roots, and rust. No wonder some of our islands look so old!

Erosion means the process of wearing away. Wind and water are the two main forces of nature that cause Hawai'i's islands to erode.

Trade winds blow toward the islands from the east. Hawai'i's high mountain peaks block the passing wind, causing clouds to gather and rain to fall on the land. Down come the wonderful tropical rains that make our islands so lush and green.

Heavy rains help the plants grow, but they also play an important role in shaping the islands. The heaviest rains fall on the eastern sides of mountains, where the rain clouds gather. Much of this water finds its way into streams and rivers. Canyons and valleys are formed as streams break down rocks that have already been weakened by roots, rain, and rust. Heavy rain can cause large chunks of land to fall away in mudslides and landslides. Rain also works with gravity to pull soil and plant life very slowly downhill toward the sea.

Eventually, even high ridges between valleys are worn down by wind, waves, and fresh water—forming cliffs called "pali" in Hawaiian. When several ridges between valleys are worn down, beautiful long pali are created. Examples of these long pali can be seen on all the islands, including the famous Nā Pali Coast on Kaua'i and the Ko'olau Pali on O'ahu.

Cliffs formed by massive chunks of land falling into the sea and the steady nibbling of ocean waves, sit at the mouths of valleys that were carved by streams. These cliffs and valleys combine to form the beautiful Nā Pali Coast, on Kaua'i.

Waipi'o Valley, Hawai'i, was formed at a time when the sea level was nearly 300 feet lower than it is today. The walls of the valley were carved mainly by streams. The wide, flat floor of the valley was formed as sediments (mug, sand, etc.) were left there by rivers and possibly by the sea.

Changes in sea level have also contributed to the changing look of the Hawaiian Islands over time. Several times in the history of the Earth, the climate has gotten so cold that enormous amounts of water throughout the world were frozen into ice as glaciers. With so much of the earth's water locked up as ice, sea levels around the world were hundreds of feet lower than they are today. Between these periods of great cold, the earth also experienced warm periods, when the ice melted and the sea level was much higher than it is today. Canyons and valleys throughout the Hawaiian Islands still hold the remains of ancient corals, shells, and river mud that settled there while these areas were beneath the sea.

Along some shorelines, huge portions of land have collapsed into the sea, leaving steep sea cliffs such as those along the Nā Pali Coast of Kauaʻi and the north shore of Molokaʻi. Slow changes occur as pounding ocean waves nibble away at the coastline, gradually shaping cliffs that grow larger as waves cause chunk after chunk of land to fall into the sea. Ocean waves and currents along the shore also wash away soil and create flat benches and sloping beaches of small rocks, shells, and bits of coral. Today, the signs of ancient shorelines can be seen in the rocks of some cliffs as colored bands of pebbles or coral. Some of these bands are hundreds of feet above the present sea level!

Gravity is one of several factors that causes an island to sink over time. How can an island "sink" when it is the tip of a mountain that already sits on the sea floor? A massive mountain of solid rock creates a great thickening in the earth's lithosphere. This spot is much heavier than the surrounding lithosphere. Scientists believe the extra weight of this thickened lithosphere, resting on the soft asthenosphere, causes the sea floor beneath the mountain to sink slightly over time. As the sea floor sinks, the island sinks as well.

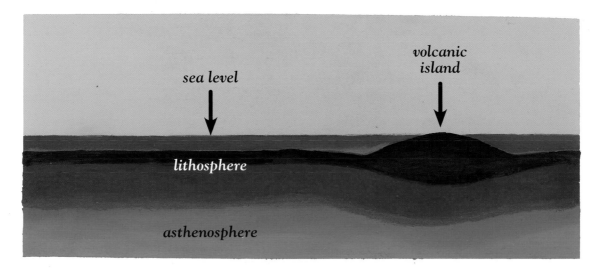

All that remains of the volcano that built French Frigate Shoals is a chunk of rock called La Perouse Pinnacle surrounded by coral reef.

THE OLD ISLAND CHANGES FACE: CORAL ATOLLS AND GUYOTS

After millions of years, the volcanic mountains of Hawai'i's islands are no longer high enough to block clouds and cause them to release rain. As the clouds pass by undisturbed and rainfall decreases, the islands become drier. Without enough rain, rivers and streams disappear, along with the lush tropical forests. When streams and forests vanish, so do the plants and animals that needed them to survive. As wind and weather continue their work, the mountains are worn down into low, dry hills. Kaua'i, with its many flowing streams and waterfalls, is the oldest of Hawai'i's high islands. The islands older than Kaua'i—Ni'ihau and the Northwestern Hawaiian Islands—are all small, low, and dry.

In time, each Hawaiian island will be reduced to a chunk of lava rock peaking above the ocean, with a few plants, insects, and birds living on it. Eventually, no traces of basalt will be left above the ocean. Yet, even this is not quite the end of the island.

While wind and waves slowly wear away the island above sea level, another kind of island-building is going on beneath the waves. Soon after the volcano rose above the sea, small coral animals settled on the warm, shallow slopes of the island and began building corals. Reef-building corals are tiny animals that live together in a shared skeleton. Growing at a rate of about an inch a year, their shared skeletons slowly form great masses of white coral rock. Coral animals live only at the surface of their shared skeletons. Over time, they build new skeletons on top of the old, leaving behind a growing mass of limestone rock. While corals grow slowly, types of rock-like algae, called "coralline algae," grow quickly and add to the structure of the coral reef.

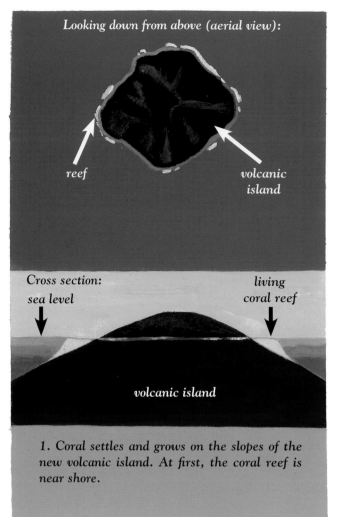

Looking down from above (aerial view):

reef   volcanic island

Cross section: sea level   living coral reef

volcanic island

1. Coral settles and grows on the slopes of the new volcanic island. At first, the coral reef is near shore.

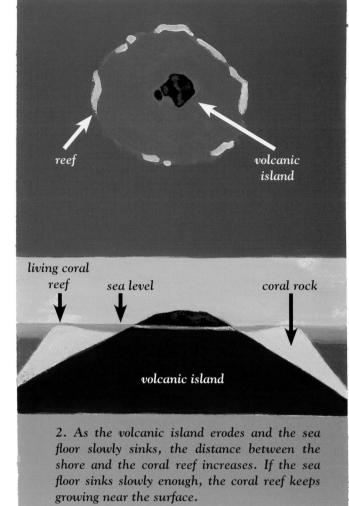

Looking down from above (aerial view):

reef   volcanic island

living coral reef   sea level   coral rock

volcanic island

2. As the volcanic island erodes and the sea floor slowly sinks, the distance between the shore and the coral reef increases. If the sea floor sinks slowly enough, the coral reef keeps growing near the surface.

As the living corals continue to grow upward toward the sun, sand and the skeletons of plants and animals that live on the reef fill in among the old coral skeletons. In this way an ever-increasing mass of solid coral rock is created.

As the island erodes and slowly sinks, it becomes smaller and the distance between the reef and shore becomes wider. The original volcanic island, now just a chunk of basalt, is surrounded by a patchy ring of coral reef. When the wind and waves have finally washed away all traces of the original basalt island, only a ring of low coral islands, called an "atoll," remains. In the Northwestern Hawaiian Islands, Nihoa and Necker still show remains of the original volcanic mountain. Farther northwest, French Frigate Shoals has almost become a coral atoll. And farther still, Maro Reef, Midway, and Kure are among several atolls that make up the last of the Hawaiian Island chain.

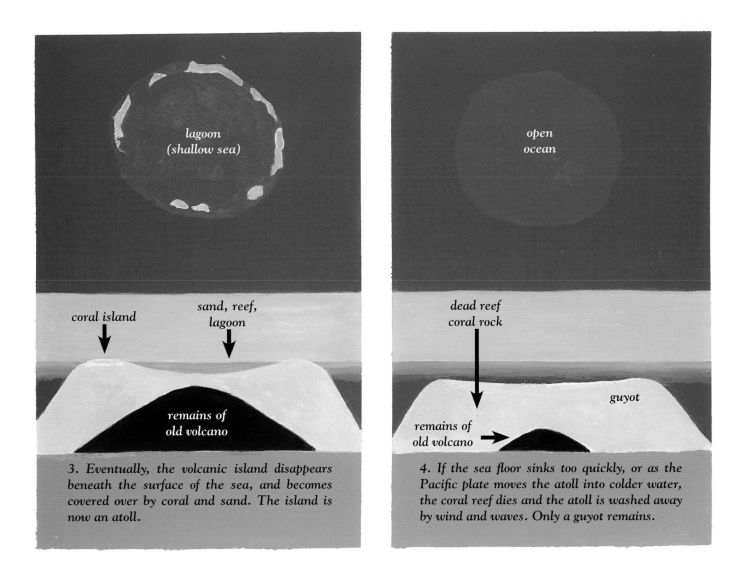

lagoon
(shallow sea)

coral island

sand, reef,
lagoon

remains of
old volcano

3. Eventually, the volcanic island disappears beneath the surface of the sea, and becomes covered over by coral and sand. The island is now an atoll.

open ocean

dead reef coral rock

guyot

remains of old volcano

4. If the sea floor sinks too quickly, or as the Pacific plate moves the atoll into colder water, the coral reef dies and the atoll is washed away by wind and waves. Only a guyot remains.

Ideally, the volcanic island sinks slowly enough for the surrounding coral reef to keep pace with it. In Hawai'i, coral reefs grow upward at a rate of less than an inch a year. If the island sinks at that rate, the reef can remain alive near the surface and maintain the atoll. But, even under these perfect conditions, the atoll cannot exist forever. As the earth's crust continues to move and the Pacific plate continues its journey to the northwest, the atoll is eventually carried into colder waters, where the coral dies. When the dead reef no longer remains at the surface, the atoll becomes a guyot (gee'o)—a sunken, flat-topped mountain rimmed with dead coral reef. The island is no more.

A round volcanic island under perfect conditions would create a round atoll, because the coral reefs follow the shape of the shore. But, because few volcanic islands are round and conditions are rarely perfect, most coral atolls are not round and do not form perfect rings.

THE FUTURE:
ISLAND UNDER THE SEA

Compared with our own lives, the life span of an island is long indeed. How amazing it is to realize that, after several million years, the tall mountains of Kaua'i and O'ahu will be completely worn down. One day, these entire islands with their lush forests and rushing streams will be nothing more than small reefs, barely showing above the waves.

The process of change is endless. We have seen how life on a new island slowly increases and multiplies into a rich variety of life forms. Over time, that same life slowly withdraws. But, just as new life springs up when old life dies, new islands are born as the old ones pass away. Even as you read the pages of this book, a new island is preparing to be born just southeast of Hawai'i island. Although the volcano is still beneath the water, it has already been given the name Lō'ihi. Lō'ihi is about fifteen miles long and eight miles wide. No one alive today will see Lō'ihi rising above the ocean waves, but scientists believe that in about 60,000 years Lō'ihi will reach above the sea and take Hawai'i's place as the youngest island in the Hawaiian chain.

Lō'ihi is rising to take its place as the newest member of the Emperor-Seamount Hawaiian Island chain. The volcano, Lō'ihi, will pass through many changes brought about by eruptions and erosion. It will see the arrival and departure of many forms of life, and will eventually sink again beneath the sea. As Lō'ihi is carried farther northwest on the moving Pacific plate, it will follow all the other Hawaiian Islands as they slide, one by one, beneath the earth's crust and are melted back into the magma that formed them. This is not the end of life. Rather, it is a small story in the endless renewal of life, as it appears and disappears in all its many changing forms.

A CLOSER VIEW:

HAWAI'I

Hawai'i, the youngest and largest of the Hawaiian Islands, is made of five volcanoes. Scientists estimate that Hawai'i rose from the sea about half a million years ago. Its highest volcano, Mauna Kea, reaches nearly 14,000 feet above the sea, making Hawai'i the highest of the Hawaiian Islands. If measured from its base on the sea floor, making it the highest mountain in the world.

During the winter months, the top of Mauna Kea is often covered with snow, and people go there to ski and sled. On the western, dry side of Mauna Kea, erosion is not very noticeable. But, on the northeastern side, where the trade winds blow in from the sea and clouds dump much rain, deep canyons and gulches have been carved out of the mountain by wind and water.

Mauna Loa is the second largest volcano on Hawai'i. Over the last one hundred years, Mauna Loa has erupted almost once every four years. In the past, lava flows from Mauna Loa have come very close to the city of Hilo, and scientists predict that someday the lava from Mauna Loa might flow right into Hilo Harbor.

Today, Kīlauea is the most active volcano on Hawai'i island. Lava has been flowing from Kīlauea almost non-stop since 1983. On almost any day of the year, visitors can stand along the shore at dusk and watch the red glow of lava as it flows into the sea, building new land.

Aia lā 'o Pele i Hawai'i eā
Ke ha'a maila i Maukele eā

There is Pele in Hawai'i
Dancing at Maukele

—traditional Hawaiian chant

33

MAUI, MOLOKAʻI, LĀNAʻI, KAHOʻOLAWE

Maui and Molokaʻi were each formed by two volcanoes, while Lānaʻi and Kahoʻolawe were each formed by a single volcano. If we could lower the sea level far enough, however, we would see that the volcanoes that formed these four islands are all part of one big mountain. Because ocean covers the low-lying land that joins the islands together, we see the four highest parts of a single land mass as four separate islands.

The tallest peak in the group of islands belongs to Haleakalā volcano on East Maui. Haleakalā rises approximately 10,000 feet above the sea. According to Hawaiian legend, the Polynesian hero Maui went to the top of Haleakalā to lasso the sun in order to slow down its journey across the sky. Many people go to the top of Haleakalā today, not to lasso the sun but to watch the breathtaking beauty of sunrise.

Traveling from sea level up the mountain slopes of Haleakalā, we pass from warm tropical beaches and coconut palms, through sugar cane and pineapple fields, up through pastures and cool evergreen forests misted by clouds, and finally above the clouds to a cold and strangely beautiful lava desert. Reds, golden browns, and rusty oranges mix with soft purples, grays, and black to create an extraordinary landscape that reminds us of the moon.

Haleakalā's crater is extremely large, but it is not a true caldera. After the volcano was formed, stream erosion and possibly glaciers formed a large depression running across the top of Haleakalā. Then, volcanic activity began again, forming cinder cones and lava flows. Thus, the crater we see today was formed through a combination of volcanic activity and stream erosion.

Kilakila ʻo Haleakalā
Kuahiwi nani o Maui

Majestic is Haleakalā
Beautiful mountain of Maui

—*traditional Hawaiian chant*

35

O'AHU

A Hawaiian kupuna, or elder, might tell us that O'ahu was formed by a brother and sister who lived on islands that were very close—but not close enough. The brother and sister wanted so badly to be together that they reached out their arms until they could touch each other and clasp hands. Then, they pulled and pulled until finally they made the two islands come together as one.

Scientists tell us that O'ahu was created three to four million years ago by two volcanoes which, as they grew larger, joined to form one island. The Wai'anae Mountain Range, to the west, is all that is left of the oldest volcano. The Ko'olau Mountains, to the east, are the remains of the second, younger volcano. After more than a million years, volcanic activity began again, creating new features on the land.

Perhaps the most famous landmark in all of Hawai'i is Diamond Head. Diamond Head was created by a violent volcanic explosion that occurred more than one million years after the Ko'olau volcano became quiet. When sea water entered a crack filled with magma, the magma's intense heat turned the water to steam. The pressure created by the rapidly expanding steam blasted through coral reef, sending great quantities of limestone, ash, and pellets of hard lava flying through the air. Punchbowl Crater, Koko Head, Koko Crater, and Hanauma Crater were also created by violent explosions caused by a mixture of sea water and magma.

The volcanic tuff cone, named Lae'ahi by the Hawaiians, was nicknamed "Diamond Head" by British sailors in 1825. It is a landmark that is recognized throughout the world.

O‘ahu, ka ‘ōnohi o nā kai　　　　　*O‘ahu, gem of the seas*

—traditional Hawaiian chant

KAUA'I AND NI'IHAU

Deep beneath the ocean, the separate islands of Ni'ihau and Kaua'i are joined as part of one great mountain. Scientists estimate that Kaua'i was formed nearly six million years ago, and that Ni'ihau is even older. The higher land on the eastern side of Ni'ihau is all that remains of the volcano that built the island. The flat, low parts of Ni'ihau developed as wind-blown sand covered dead coral reef. The reef grew below the ocean, but died as lowering sea levels left it exposed to the air.

Kaua'i was formed by a single volcano, whose caldera was about thirteen miles across. Although this is the largest in the world, it is difficult to recognize because of the many changes brought by time. The volcano that formed Kaua'i rested for more than a million years, while wind, rain, and waves left their mark on the land. Then, the volcano became active again, spreading new lava over parts of the already eroded land.

Kaua'i is famous for its natural beauty. Majestic mountains carved by streams and sparkling waterfalls glow green and gold in the setting sun. Pale sand beaches and black rocky coasts encircle Kaua'i like a colorful lei. It isn't surprising that Kaua'i is chosen as the setting for many movies.

The beauty of Kaua'i comes from her age. Sharp, wrinkled mountains, deep canyons, sea caves, and the stunning Nā Pali Coast are a few of Kaua'i's natural treasures, formed over time by wind and water.

Waimea Canyon, one of Kaua'i's major landmarks, was created by land shifts called "faults," and by flowing water. Also called "The Grand Canyon of the Pacific," the canyon rocks glow at sunset in shades of rusty orange, brick red, soft purple and gray.

Maika‘i Kaua‘i
Hemolele ika mālie

Kaua‘i is very good
Majestic in the calm

—traditional Hawaiian chant

THE NORTHWESTERN HAWAIIAN ISLANDS

Farther to the northwest, the Hawaiian Island chain continues as a string of low, dry islands, shallow seas, and coral reefs. Generally, these islands are not visited by people, but are home to Hawaiian monk seals, sea turtles, and a variety of sea birds.

The islands nearer to Kaua'i—Ka'ula, Nihoa, Necker, French Frigate Shoals, and Gardner—have been so worn down over time that they are little more than chunks of volcanic rock. Scientists think Nihoa is over 7 million years old and Necker is about 11 million years old. French Frigate Shoals and Gardner have hardly any volcanic rock left above sea level, and are surrounded by coral reef.

The islands farthest to the north-west—Maro Reef, Laysan, Lisianski, Pearl and Hermes Reff, Midway, and Kure—are all atolls. Their coral reef and limestone islands cover the submerged remains of old shield volcanoes. For more than a hundred years, scientists believed that these coral islands rested on sunken volcanic mountains. Only recently, they have been able to drill holes down through the coral rock, bringing up samples of basalt and proving that their ideas were correct.

Laysan atoll is a flat, coral island surrounded by reefs. It is all that remains of a volcanic island, now sunken beneath the sea. Like many of the Northwestern Hawaiian Islands, Laysan is a home and refuge for wildlife, including the Laysan albatross, the Laysan duck, and the Laysan finch.

40

ISLAND ENERGY: A HOT SUBJECT OF DEBATE

It takes a lot of energy to create a volcanic explosion. Is there a way that people can control and use this energy? In some parts of the world where volcanic activity creates heat beneath the ground, people dig deep wells into the hot earth and pump water into the wells. The heated water turns into steam, which is used to generate electricity. This source of energy is called "geothermal," meaning earth-heat.

Today, many countries are looking for cheap, safe ways to make electricity. On the island of Hawai'i, several geothermal wells have been dug to test the use of geothermal energy for making electricity. Some people like it; others think it does more harm than good.

People who support the use of geothermal energy in Hawai'i claim it is cleaner for the environment than energy from either coal or oil. They believe geothermal energy will cost less and will free us from the need for supplies of oil, which is quickly being used up. People who are against using geothermal energy in Hawai'i point out that Hawaiian rain forest must be cut down to make roads and build sites for geothermal plants. This would destroy many delicate plants and animals living in the forest, some of which live nowhere else on earth. Additionally, the steam from geothermal plants is full of sulfur and other chemicals. High enough levels of sulfur gas are dangerous to breathe, and many people became afraid for their health when there are leaks from test wells. Unlike the test well, the power plant that operates today runs very quietly almost all of the time and is self-contained so the sulphurous steam is not released into the air.

Many modern Hawaiians still practice the ancient Hawaiian religion. They worship the goddess Pele and believe her lands and volcanoes to be sacred. They feel it shows deep disrespect to dig into Pele's mountain and take the volcano's energy without her permission.

Like other issues today, the question of whether or not to use geothermal energy in Hawai'i has no clear-cut answer. It is important for Hawai'i's young people to study and understand this complex issue, because one day they will be active in making decisions about geothermal energy and Hawai'i's future.

Coral reefs are part of the island system. Living coral reefs protect the land from erosion, caused by pounding waves, and allow the island to develop into an atoll. Soil and fresh water flowing off the land kill some corals. Although this is a natural process, human activities on land have greatly speeded up the destruction of reef and the erosion of our islands.

CARING FOR THE LAND

Historians think that the Polynesians first came to Hawai'i less than two thousand years ago. What does this mean in "island time?" If you imagine the four-million-year-old island of O'ahu to be just one day old, it means people arrived only during the last thirty seconds.

Although people are newcomers to Hawai'i, we are causing erosion to speed up drastically on the islands where we live. How? By the way we treat the land.

People brought farming animals to Hawai'i many years ago. Grazing goats and sheep that eat the grass and other plants have caused major erosion on parts of all the islands. Plant roots hold down the soil and plant leaves slow down the rain as it falls to the ground, helping it soak into the soil instead of rushing across the surface. When this blanket of roots and leaves is removed, either by animals or by clearing land for farming or to build roads and houses, soil quickly washes away. You can see this along Hawai'i's highways. Many highways have been cut through hills, leaving steep hillsides of red earth on each side of the road. Some cut hillsides are covered with soft mesh and grass seed that help new plants grow and hold the soil. Other hillsides are left open to bleed red earth with each heavy rain.

Storm drains and concrete canals have been built to help protect homes and businesses from flooding during heavy rains. Although the purpose of storm drains and canals is to get rainwater to the sea as quickly as possible, the fast-flowing water also carries soil and chemicals from plantation farming and golf courses into the ocean. Unfortunately, by making fresh water flow into the sea faster, we are killing coral reefs. To correct this, the government requires the plantations to dig special ponds that capture storm water before it rushes into the sea. Mud settles to the bottom of the ponds and is dug out and dumped back onto the land, instead of onto the reef.

Coral reefs protect Hawai'i's shorelines from pounding waves. If they die, our islands will erode much faster. Without living coral reefs, the Hawaiian Islands cannot become atolls. As we have seen, coral reefs are killed by fresh water, along with the mud and chemicals it often carries. Coral reefs are also killed by people who walk on them. Tourists walking across reef flats, either to look at them or to get into boats anchored offshore, damage and kill corals. One person walking on a reef one time won't cause a big problem, but many people, day after day, walking on—or even touching—coral reefs cause great damage.

WHAT YOU CAN DO TO HELP:

In Hawai'i, people have speeded up erosion in an unnatural way. Fortunately, people can also slow down erosion. You can help. Here's how:

- Don't drive cars along the beach dunes. The dunes and plants growing on them protect the beach.

- Do keep plants and trees covering the soil around your yard.

- Don't take rocks from the shoreline or sand from the beach.

- Do become aware of public issues concerning land use and water use (for example, roadside spraying to kill weeds, storm drainage problems, and chemicals from farming and golf courses).

- Don't wash any chemicals down a storm drain. Whatever goes down a storm drain washes directly to the sea.

- Do send clean water into areas with growing plants instead of down storm drains whenever you can.

- Don't walk on coral reefs or touch living coral.

- Do think of protecting the entire coastline when building a sea wall, rather than just protecting a small piece of land.

GLOSSARY

'A'Ā a type of lava that looks like gravel. A flowing stream of pāhoehoe may turn into 'a'ā as it cools, so 'a'ā is usually found below flows of pāhoehoe on the mountain.

ASTHENOSPHERE the layer of Earth which lies below the lithosphere, from 60 to 215 miles below the surface. The asthenosphere is composed of soft, partially melted rock.

ATOLL a flat, ring-shaped coral island, or group of islands, which surrounds shallow ocean water called a lagoon. Mountainous volcanic islands may become flat atolls after millions of years of erosion and coral growth.

BASALT dark volcanic rock. Basalt is made up of different minerals including feldspar, pyroxine, and olivine. When basalt becomes so hot that it melts, it will flow a very long distance before it cools and hardens.

CALCIUM CARBONATE a white mineral. The skeletons of coral, coralline algae, and the shells of many reef animals are all made of calcium carbonate.

CORAL small marine animals whose skeletons form rock-like structures that are also called corals. Corals grow in oceans around the world, but they only form coral reefs in warm, shallow oceans.

CORAL REEFS large deposits of coral rock built by corals and coral-like plants in tropical seas where the water is clear and shallow enough for the corals to receive sunlight. A dead coral reef may consist of only coral rock, while a living coral reefs contains many plants and animals living among the corals.

ERUPTION a sudden outburst or explosion that happens when pressure underground builds up so much that steam and hot rocks burst out from the earth's crust.

GLACIER a large amount of ice formed on land which flows downhill like a very slow-moving river. Glaciers form in very cold places where snow falls faster than snow melts.

GRAVITY a force which pulls everything on the earth towards the center of the earth. Because of gravity, human beings can walk and stand on the earth's surface without floating away into outer space.

GUYOT a sunken flat-topped mountain beneath the sea.

LAVA the name given to magma once magma comes out from below the earth's surface. Lava is usually in a liquid form when it first comes out of the volcano but even after it hardens it is still called lava.

LIMESTONE a kind of rock composed mostly of calcium carbonate, the same material that coral reefs are made of.

LITHOSPHERE the relatively hard, rigid, outer layer of the Earth which includes the crust and the part of the mantle laying above the asthenosphere.

MAGMA hot, melted rock that is found within the earth's crust.

PĀHOEHOE a type of smooth, shiny lava that looks like cake batter as it is being poured into the pan. When lava first flows out of the mountain it is usually pāhoehoe.

STALACTITES look like icicles made of rock. Stalactites form in lava tubes as hot lava drips from the ceiling. Lava drips harden one on top of another other until they form a long icicle of hardened lava.

TRADE WINDS winds that blow steadily in tropical areas. Due to the spinning of the earth, trade winds always blow from an easterly direction.

INDEX